A BRIEF HISTORY OF THE New England Historic-Genealogical Society,

READ AT THE

MONTHLY MEETING, MAY 7, 1862,

BY J. H. SHEPPARD, A. M.,

LIBRARIAN OF THE SOCIETY.

ALBANY:
J. MUNSELL, 78 STATE STREET.
1862.

A BRIEF HISTORY.

"The time will come, sir, when it will be accounted an honor to have descended from the men, who first settled this country."—*Address*, 1852, *by the Rev. William Jenks, D. D., Hon. Memb.*

Every association, institute or political body, like a human being, as it progresses to maturity, has its infancy, youth and manhood. It has been so with our Genealogical Society; at first feeble, then vigorous and now strong and flourishing. A brief outline of our history seems peculiarly adapted to our situation and wants at the present time.

The preliminary steps toward the formation of this Society occurred at the residence of William H. Montague, merchant of Boston, in Orange street, Oct. 1844; which were followed by a meeting at Mr. Shattuck's, No. 79 Harrison Avenue, on Friday evening Nov. 1, of the same year. The gentlemen then present were Charles Ewer, Samuel G. Drake, William H. Montague, J. Wingate Thornton and Lemuel Shattuck. They organized the meeting and chose Mr. Ewer President and Mr. Thornton Secretary. It may be asked, who first conceived the idea of an institution which in 17 years from its incorporation has grown into such magnitude and influence? For we may rest assured that no invention, discovery or useful project ever took place without a thought from some prime mover, or a suggestion first made by an original thinker.

The answer to this question may be rendered certain, and will be only an act of justice to the memory of a worthy and excellent man. Charles Ewer was the first mover and originator of a plan which led to the formation of the "N. E. Historic-Genealogical Society," which he wished to be entitled the "N. E. Genealogical and Heraldic Society." He was a man of leisure, was anxious to form such an association and invited congenial spirits to unite with him in this object. It was a grand and noble thought; for this Genealogical Society is the first one, particularly devoted to the Pedigree of families in the world. Some years after, a similar society was instituted at London. We know of no other. Perhaps the lamented Charles Ewer, when he first meditated in the secret chamber of his brain, on the formation of a Society so valuable, felt like that quaint and pious poet of old England, Herbert, when he said,

"He that good thinketh, good may do,
For God will help him thereunto;
For was never good work wrought
Without beginning of good thought."

In December, the Constitution, which had been drafted by a Committee, was adopted. March 18, 1845, an Act of Incorporation was granted by the Legislature, wherein the object of this Society was set forth in these words: "For the purpose of collecting, preserving, and occasionally publishing genealogical and historical matter, relating to early New England families, and for the establishment of a Cabinet." This great aim was also emphatically represented in a Circular by the Directors, June, 1847; that is, to RESCUE THE DECAYING RECORDS OF NEW ENGLAND. These words were not a mere flourish of the pen; for a quarterly was published by the Society, young and comparatively feeble as it was; and No. 1, of the *New England Historical and Genealogical Register* was issued Jan. 1, 1847, under the editorial care of the late Rev. William Cogswell, D. D.

We have described the Birth of our Society; let us for a moment look at its struggles in Infancy. It began in poverty. No rich patron, nor beneficent donor smiled on it as it stretched out its little arms. Its nursery was a solitary chamber, No. 9, in the third story of the "City Building," so called, Court Square; an out-of-the-way place, small, being only 12 feet square, badly lighted from back windows overlooking a dark alley—a room, indeed sombre enough and poorly adapted to the wants of the little Genealogical stranger. An old table, troubled with the podagra—a chair or two which had seen better days—and a set of pine shelves without back or panel, subject to the rickets; such was the furniture in this cavernous-looking spot—this Pandora's box with only hope at the bottom. But as the Society held their meetings for business in the attic room of the Am. Ed. Soc., in Cornhill, this dark chamber was resorted to rather as a place for depositing donations. The amount of these donations for the year 1845, as appears by the Records, will show how small was that beginning which formed a nucleus around which have gathered in sixteen years so many golden treasures of antiquarian research. There were presented in 1845, 24 bound volumes of books—10 manuscripts—6 plans—an old lease—4 bound volumes of the Independent Chronicle, 1804–1811—and 185 pamphlets, consisting of sermons, catalogues, orations and miscellaneous matter *De omnibus rebus et quibusdam aliis;* besides, "a wheelbarrow load of manuscript sermons"—as the record has it—"of Dr. Joseph Eckley, Old South Church." The books were scattered on the shelves; but these pamphlets of the infant Society, lay like swaddling clothes in a corner, where it slept.

To follow its growth and progress year by year, would be unprofitable and only weary the reader's patience. Daily records have been kept wherein the donations and donors' names are preserved, with all the proceedings, and deposited in our archives. The ghostly chamber in the City Building was abandoned Oct. 6, 1847, for a room larger and a little better, but still badly windowed, on the first floor in Massachusetts Block, No. 8. This building was then a kind of Lincoln's Inn, and the little fellow got nestled among the lawyers. Some furniture was procured with cases and shelves, and the donations soon began to accumulate and make a show of antiquity where they stood carefully arranged.

During the three or more years this tenebrious place was occupied, our prospects were slowly and hopefully encouraging; until Jan. 1851, a new room was hired, more lightsome and pleasant, No. 5 Tremont Row; and here to continue our similitude, the Society passed its youth; for this room was occupied nearly seven years, until the shelves, cases and walls were so crowded, with books pamphlets, MSS., newspapers, portraits, &c., that the growing society had but a small space to meet in, and a bibliothecal stevedore would have found it difficult with a cotton-screw to press more donations into any part of the library. Another and a better apartment, No. 13, Bromfield street—our present large and well lighted hall—was secured for our use in Oct. 1858, and any one who knows how small in size the Society once was, and now looks around on the numerous shelves and cases for books, and closets for manuscripts, which are all well filled, must acknowledge that it has reached the full stature of manhood, and well deserves the "freedom suit" of some fire-proof building.

Before contemplating the Library, it may be well to cast our eye on the annual increase of resident members. Beginning with 1844, when there were only 5 original members, the statistical table stands thus:

	New Members.		New Members.		New Members.
1845,........	37	1851,........	22	1857,........	43
1846,........	21	1852,........	21	1858,........	71
1847,........	32	1853,........	40	1859, ...	60
1848,...	14	1854,........	12	1860,........	46
1849,........	2	1855,........	40	1861,........	20
1850,........	22	1856,........	30		

The Society now consists of about 325 paying members; in addition to which there is a large number of Corresponding and Honorary members. The Presidents were as follows: Charles Ewer, Esq., Jan. 1845–1850; Rev. Joseph B. Felt, LL. D., 1850–1853; William Whiting, Esq., 1853–1858; Samuel G. Drake, A. M., 1858–1859; Almon D. Hodges, Esq., 1859–1861; and Winslow Lewis, M. D., 1861, President at this time.

By the Report of Frederic Kidder, Esq., Chairman of the Library Committee, Jan. 1, 1862, it appears that there are over 5,000 bound volumes of books, and about 18,000 pamphlets of various kinds belonging to the library. A Catalogue of the books has been made within a year.

Many of the books are very valuable, and if lost could not be replaced. For instance twenty large folio volumes, well bound, of the U. S. Direct Tax of 1798, in Massachusetts, including Maine then a district. This gigantic work, containing nearly every town, is all but complete. Three vols. have each a copious index—the rest need one. This Domesday-book of the Bay-State is of inestimable value to the genealogist and biographer of New England. In addition to numerous plans and ancient charts and a great collection of Mss., some of which are very old and rare, the Society has 94 bound volumes of pedigrees and about 133 distinct family lists of ancestors, included in separate pamphlets or in volumes—making all together at least 227 genealogies of different families; also 102 volumes of town histories, which include pedigrees not elsewhere published. Many of these pedigrees are noticed in that recent and exceedingly useful *Hand book of American Genealogy*, by William H. Whitmore, a member of our Society. It is a source of no small satisfaction to the N. E. His.-Gen. Soc., while it has been struggling through many difficulties and discouragements, to behold on its shelves no small number of these pedigrees and town histories and kindred works which were written and published by some of its own members. The same remark might also apply to some of our books on biography. A tree is known by its fruit, and a Society like ours by its genealogical trees.

It may be here observed, that in the General Statutes of Mass., chap. 18, sec. 10, p. 158, there is a provision that towns in this commonwealth may grant and vote such sums as they may think necessary, "For procuring the writing and publishing their town histories." This clause was re-enacted from an act of April 29, 1854, chap. 429; a law got up by the writer of this article, when he was a member of the Legislature. Its utility was then so apparent, that it passed the House unanimously without comment. It is said that in Vermont a similar statute soon followed.

There is also in the library a choice collection of works on Heraldry; Rymer's *Fœdera* in 19 great folios; a very curious old book, the *Andreæ Lectura*, an antique on Genealogy, in Latin, printed about 1474 at Nuremberg, perhaps the earliest printed volume on Pedigree, illuminated by hand and with a pictured model of a genealogical tree, with the motto *Sequit figura arboris consanguinitatis;* and several elaborate histories of English counties. Nor would I forget to mention the beautiful specimen of music, 650 pages on parchment or vellum, presented by Col. Swett, to whom it was sent by his daughter at Florence. It is a Roman Catholic choral book, and by Bishop Fitzpatrick was called a Graduale. The musical notes are square or angular, different from those now in use. On each page are letters splendidly illuminated. There can be no doubt that it is the work of a pen before the invention of printing, which was about 1440; therefore it must be nearly 500 years old, if not more. It is a beautiful curiosity, and the chants on those pages now silent as death, must have once awakened the sweetest feelings of adoration in the Italian chapel or cathedral their melody filled.

There is a large collection of MSS., some of which are of early date in the settlement of the country; such as Hull's *Journal* written in 1675, and Russell's *Treasury Accounts of Massachusetts Bay*, 1645–1656.

Among the donors whose names appear on our records, reference should be made to the liberality of Charles Ewer and William Whiting, our past Presidents—to the Hon. Edward Everett, who in March 1852, donated more than 100 volumes—to the Hon. David Sears for some costly works he procured for the Society from London—to the late Hon. Nathan Appleton for some rare and valuable volumes—and for several hundreds of books, many of them scarce and ancient, besides a mass of old MSS. and pamphlets, from Dr. Lewis. The heart that is warmed with grateful emotions delights to speak of its benefactors. And we would not forget the generous bequest of the late Dr. Henry Bond of Philadelphia—of which an account is given in a Memoir of him in the *N. E. His.-Gen. Reg.*, vol. XIV, p. 1–3—which bequest has been invested in the "Bond Fund." Nor would we be silent on the two donations of John Barstow, Esq., of Providence, R. I., which are to form a permanent fund. Mention should also be made of a rich gift from the British Government, viz. The Rotuli, or Rolls of Parliament and Record Publications of Great Britain, being 29 volumes principally folios; and also of a large number of its publications, including three great folio volumes of Plates sent us by the London Society of Antiquaries.

Since I began to take charge of this library—nearly a year and a half ago—I have been surprised at the number of gentlemen who have come here to look up their pedigrees. One from Oregon, another from California, another from Illinois, and numbers from the middle states, and different parts of New England, have called and spent hours and some few even days, in searching genealogy and heraldry, taking minutes, and pondering over the faint or certain traces of their ancestors. Not long since two very civil and intelligent Mormons from Utah spent some hours in searching their progenitors and went away somewhat pleased at the information they obtained. Letters of inquiry, touching this subject are not unfrequent. It shows the value of our association, and the increasing spread of its influence; and let it be our grand object and untiring effort to obtain every book of pedigree, and everything touching this subject in New England, that our Genealogical Society may be the HEAD-QUARTERS, from which shall issue all true knowledge of New England ancestry.

But among the respectable, and sometimes eminent visitors to our Genealogical Library, in search of their family history, there is one class of a different kind, which deserves no encouragement and ought to be repudiated as drones in the hive of human society. I refer to hunters of English fortunes—weak men, led on by speculators to false hopes and great expectations, and deluded into a notion that some rich old fellow of the same name—some hundreds of years ago—died without children, and an immense inheritance has slept in abeyance, till the lost heir turns up in a cottage under the cliffs of New England.

Such infatuation is of a similar character with the dreams of money diggers; and from the great faith of some of the dupes in finding hidden treasures, it would seem that Herman Dousterswivel in Walter Scott's inimitable *Antiquary* when he dug for ingots among the ruins of St. Ruth, was no fiction, but a reality. So many rogues have deluded the credulous in this way, and so much imposition has been practised by hungry sharpers on each side of the Atlantic, that the best way is to turn a cold shoulder to all hunters of inheritances and advise them to waste no money on agents and go to work.

The regular reading of papers before the Society at their monthly meetings began in February, 1855, at the suggestion of our former vigilant and active Librarian, the Rev. Luther Farnham, who delivered in October of that year a very interesting article—which was afterwards published under the title of a *Glance at Private Libraries.* Several of the Readings have been printed in a pamphlet form, and in magazines and newspapers—a particular reference to which the time forbids; although the valuable paper on New England Architecture by the Rev. N. H. Chamberlain, deserves your attention. Some of the Readings have been marked by a talent and learning which would have delighted a large assembly of the public, as they did our limited audience;—a convincing proof that we need a Lecture-room to accommodate a greater number and enable the Society to enlarge their invitations.

Some idea may be formed of the progress and present flourishing state of the Society by a reference to Addresses delivered at annual or public meetings, four of which have been published in the *Register* and also separately distributed in a pamphlet form. The first was by the Rev. William Jenks, D. D., March 1, 1852, in which that elegant and learned scholar and eminent linguist in his own peculiar and happy manner illustrated the connection—the *commune vinculum*—of History, Biography and Heraldry with Genealogy the great object of our institution.

The next was by William Whiting, Esq., Jan. 12, 1853, as President, in which he portrayed the purposes and design of the Society in a striking manner and great variety of particulars, pointing out in a graphic sketch the ardor and enthusiasm with which a searcher of Genealogy enters on his task, perseveres in the pursuit and after he has accomplished his object, we "hear his shout of joy when he at last finds the lost jewel." *Register*, vol. VII, p. 106.

Jan. 20, 1858, Mr. Samuel G. Drake, A. M., President of the Society, gave us another Address. He had been Corresponding Secretary thirteen years, and from his long and unwearied devotion to Antiquarian researches, his remarks were valuable and instructive, fraught with the weight of experience. "I wish"—he observes—"particularly to impress upon the minds of all present, that they should encourage contributions of books, pamphlets, as well as manuscripts of every description. For who can estimate the value a single pamphlet or letter may be to somebody at some time?" This he corroborates by an anecdote directly in point to which I must refer for want of room.

The last Address was from our President Winslow Lewis, M. D., Jan. 1, 1862. The happy and classical reference to the long hallowed customs of marking this day in the calendar of life was introduced with much effect. Nor were the allusions to the Christmas carols with "cake and ale" less touching at the time, as we were then entering upon the last half of the Holidays so dear to the recollections of many and waking up delightful thoughts of other times, as some old poet feelingly sings:

"The Chimes, the Chimes of mother land,
Of England green and old;
That out from thane and ivied tower,
A thousand years have told."

The union of Genealogy with Biography, Heraldry, Numismatics and History was set forth and exemplified fully; but there was a province of Genealogy of peculiar importance, which has seldom been brought before the notice of our Society; and coming from one of eminent professional experience it has the sanction, as it were, of a truth *ex* *cathedrâ.* It is this: "That mental as well as physical qualities are handed down more or less from parent to child, from forefathers to posterity, and that thus, pure and healthy descent is of immense importance. * * * And very frequently we can ascribe the united qualities of valor and of virtue, of great intellect and gentle heart, to the marriage union of parents, whose families were respectively distinguished for these virtues."

These four Addresses, though on subjects somewhat similar, have presented the object and aim of our Society in so many different points of view, and all concentrating in one grand purpose—the preservation of all kinds of documents from ruin—that they deserve the special attention of every member.

There is also one other Address which was delivered before the N. E. His.-Gen. Society in the Hall of the House of Representatives of Mass., September 13, 1859, and published. It was by one of our members, the Hon. Lorenzo Sabine, a Centennial Address on the death of Maj. Gen. James Wolfe, who died on the heights of Quebec in the arms of victory, Sep. 13, 1759. The subject was one of great interest, as a brilliant epoch in the Colonial history, and as a memorial of one of England's noblest warriors. Both branches of the Legislature were present, and delegations from several antiquarian and historic societies attended. Mr. Sabine's well known reputation as a writer and a most accurate investigator of facts, was ably sustained; and he has given to us a piece of Biography, rich and exceedingly interesting—a diamond of the first water. It is beautifully printed making a centurial pamphlet, of exactly 100 pages, including notes and 36 pages of Appendix.

The value and importance of the *N. E. Historical and Genealogical Register*, which commenced as a quarterly Jan. 1, 1847, and has now reached xv complete volumes—whether we regard the numerous sketches of biography, the minute and carefully drawn pedigrees of families or the fragments of the early history of our country—cannot be estimated in the bird's eye view of this article. Our *Register* has travelled on, patient, noiseless and persevering, for fifteen years in the humble path of usefulness. It has sought none of the rhetorical adornments of genius, nor the charms of fiction; nor even tried to cull a blossom on the Parnassian mountains and valleys of New England—unless it be a MAY-FLOWER, which has at times perfumed its pages. It has become a reservoir of facts, which from day to day and year to year will grow more precious. And when we, whose locks are touched with age, and all our younger members, have passed away, this ancestral monument of so many honored families—some of whom were lineal descendants of the Pilgrim Fathers—will be sought out, read and cherished, as an Englishman venerates the Armorial bearings transmitted to him by progenitors who did their country some service. This *Genealogical Register* has already been a copious fountain, from which some books of Pedigree have drawn a rich supply; nor has a generous credit always been given, where pretty large annexations of original matter have been made. But the *Register* is able to bear it and stand alone on its merit.

That we may justly appreciate the worth of this elaborate work, let us suppose for a moment that every copy of the xv volumes, was suddenly blotted out of existence, and moreover, that the learned antiquarian—the indefatigable historian of Boston—who so long and so ably conducted a large portion of the work, had gone to his rest; where could we supply their place? Who then could restore the lost pedigrees of so many New England families, which, root and branch, have been here embalmed? Their memory would perish in that deep, dark gulf over which the waters of Lethe are rolling forever! This Register of the past—even if it should stop, after the current year's experiment—which we sincerely hope may not be so, but like the Eagle it may renew its strength—will stand the test of of time, and a hundred years hence be called for and sought by descendants of the Pilgrim Fathers.

Those who undervalue a regard to Pedigree may deem these remarks as enthusiastic or visionary. They can see no beauty nor benefit in Genealogy. It was far otherwise in that ancient land, where honor to our father and mother was deemed among the first of virtues, and where the Law and the Gospel first prevailed. We are informed in Calmet's great *Dictionary of the Bible* that "the Hebrews carefully preserved their genealogies and never was a nation more circumspect respecting them." Josephus speaks of the uninterrupted succession of priests for 2,000 years; and Jerome, who wrote in the 4th century, says the Jews knew so perfectly their genealogies that they could repeat all the names from Abraham to Zerubbabel. According to the prophet Ezra, chap. ii, 62, a priest, who could not trace his genealogy, was not admitted to the ministry. In England the Herald's College is the great office where the enrolment of distinguished pedigrees is kept under the various and almost infinite emblems of a Coat of Arms, which to a stranger appears odd and trifling, but to any one who is conversant with the metals, colors and furs, the charges and crests with which a shield is emblazoned, will see the propriety and beauty of Heraldry and that it is worthy of the study it requires: for it is not learnt in a moment; it is a language by itself.

It is true that Genealogy is a dry pursuit and demands patient research, mental labor and no small skill in forming a clear and tabular view of a man's progenitors. It is a science which makes little noise, and requires a mind like Old Mortality to decipher the inscriptions on tombstones, or an antiquarian eye to sift old wills and search the natal or funeral annals of a family in their "Big ha' Bible." Who does not wish to know something of his ancestors? And more especially if he have become eminent in wealth or talent. Such a desire is a principle inherent in our nature; it is born in us, and is only lost by vice or debasing pursuits. The moment a man rises above the level of a clown or churl, he looks beyond the nameless hillocks of the dead and wishes to know where his buried ancestors lie. There are those born, it is true, *consumere fruges terræ*, who care for none of these things. But as a man advances in taste, intellectual improvement and the delight of knowledge, he grows more anxious to get some tidings of those ancestors from whom he is descended. Even the immortal Washington, it is said, used means to trace his ancestry, and they were not unsuccessful, for his descent was worthy of his fame. We may look back through ages on our progenitors, but we can only look forward for years to our posterity, for, as they are coming on the stage, we are going off. It was a beautiful thought of Virgil, but contrary to human nature, when he represents Anchises in the Elysian fields, as bringing before his son's eyes the shades of his illustrious descendants from Silvius down to Augustus Cæsar, one after another like "dissolving views." Such visions of our future progeny, perhaps, we may have from some standpoint in the celestial world, but not on this dark earth, for we know not what a day may bring forth.

When the ancients could not find a splendid parentage for a favorite hero, they solemnly averred that he was descended from some deity they worshiped. In this kind of Genealogy they made Hercules the son of Jupiter and a young lady of Argos by the name of Alcmena whom the Thunderer bewitched; Pious Æneas who carried his father out of flaming Troy on his shoulders, was the son of Anchises and Venus the queen of beauty; and Romulus and Remus were twins, the children of Mars and Miss Ilia of Alba, a vestal virgin; but, these fashionable parents left the little gemini to be suckled by a wolf. Such was the love of the Ancients for tracing their pedigree either on earth below or among the Olympian gods and goddesses above. Even in one of the late Genealogical works, the derivation of the name of the ancient stirps savors a little of a half-way connexion with Jupiter and a kind of avuncular relationship to Hercules.

Pardon this digression. It is pleasant to allude to those classic allegories which illuminated the reading of early days and sometimes give the color of the rose to the realities of life. Indeed, of a clear night I can never look upon the heavens above, without beholding the Mythology of the ancients written on the blue sky in the starry letters of the constellations.

But, it is time this sketch should draw to a close, some parts of which may seem superfluous after the subject of Genealogy has been so happily and ably handled in the recent address of our President. Yet if any thing I have said on this point should lead to a more careful perusal of that valuable document, my labor will not be in vain. One thing I can assure you, I have been induced to recommend the tracing of pedigrees to the descendants of the Pilgrim Fathers, by no self-flattering motives as it regards myself; for my ancestors and birth were in England. Yet both there and here the contemplation of the virtues of our progenitors has a tendency to make us more virtuous, and many a son has lived more nobly from the recollection that the blood which flows in his veins came from an honorable and elevated source. On the other hand the light of a distinguished ancestry will only make the spots more visible and hideous in the character of a degenerate descendant.

I have said that the N. E. His.-Gen. Society is now in its manhood; yes in strong, healthy and vigorous manhood. Is it not so? January 1, 1862, our indefatigable and excellent treasurer, William B. Towne, Esq., reported that we were out of debt. We have a large and pleasant hall to meet in, where the light from the north and south cheers the eye as it ranges up and down the library; and yet, though the rooms we occupy are much safer than are usually found in the centre of a large city like this, there is not an active member of this

Society, who does not feel anxious and insecure, like one whose cottage lies at the foot of a volcano; for if a fire should break on this spot, what would become of so many scarce books, ancient manuscripts and rare works. Their loss would be irreparable. No money could restore them.

We are told by Scott in the *Fortunes of Nigel* that in the time of James the 1st, King of England, it was the custom in London for men in trade to send out their clerks into the street, and cry out to the passers by, "*What d'ye lack? What d'ye lack?*" Should some of our merchant-princes, or millionaires put to our Society a similar question, our answer is ready:

1. We lack a Fire-proof-room to secure our rare books and manuscripts.
2. We lack a Lecture room, where the readings at our monthly meetings could be heard and better appreciated by a larger audience.
3. We lack a room for the storage of duplicates and documents, whose worth will be better known at a future day.

In a word we need a Fire-proof building; it would cost probably $20,000. One tenth or one twentieth of this amount has been already offered by a member, if nine or nineteen will join him. Who will aid in this noble undertaking?

OFFICERS

OF THE

NEW ENGLAND HISTORIC-GENEALOGICAL SOCIETY,

FROM ITS ORGANIZATION IN JANUARY, 1845, TO JUNE, 1862.

[Compiled by J. W. DEAN.]

* Prefixed to a name, signifies *deceased;* † Signifies *ex-officio.*

Presidents.

	*Charles Ewer, Esq., of Boston, Mass.,...........	Jan. 1845, to Jan. 1850
Rev.	Joseph Barlow Felt, LL.D., of Boston,...........	" 1850, to " 1853
	William Whiting, A. M.,of Roxbury, ...	" 1853, to " 1858
	Samuel Gardner Drake, A. M., of Boston,........	" 1858, to " 1859
	Almon D. Hodges, Esq., of Roxbury, Mass.,......	" 1859, to " 1861
	Winslow Lewis, M. D., of Boston,...............	" 1861.

Vice-Presidents.

	*Lemuel Shattuck, Esq., of Boston, Mass.,........	Jan. 1845, to Jan. 1850
Rev.	Lucius Robinson Paige, D. D., of Cambridge, Mass.	" 1850, to " 1851
	Nathaniel B. Shurtleff, M. D., of Boston, Mass., ..	" 1851, to " 1853
Hon.	Timothy Farrar, A. M., of Boston, Mass.,.........	" 1853, to " 1858
Hon.	William Willis, A. M., of Portland, Me.,.........	Feb. 1855, to " 1859
Hon.	Noah Martin, M. D., of Dover, N. H.,............	" 1855, to " 1859
*Rev.	John Wheeler, D. D., of Burlington, Vt.,........	" 1855, to " 1859
Hon.	William R. Staples, A. M., of Providence, R. I.,...	" 1855, to " 1859
*Hon.	Nathaniel Goodwin, of Hartford, Ct.,............	" 1855, to May 1855
Rev.	Leonard Bacon, D. D., of New Haven, Ct.,.......	Aug. 1855, to Jan. 1859
Hon.	Frances Brinley, A. M., of Boston,...............	Jan. 1858, to " 1859
Hon.	Charles Hudson, A. M., of Lexington, Mass.,......	" 1859, to " 1861
Hon.	John Appleton, of Bangor, Me.,..................	" 1859.
Hon.	Samuel D. Bell, LL.D., of Manchester, N. H.,....	" 1859.
	Henry Clark, Esq., of Poultney, Vt.,............	" 1859.
	John Barstow, Esq., of Providence, R. I.,.........	" 1859.
Rev.	F. W. Chapman, A. M., of Ellington, Ct.,........	" 1859.
Rev.	Martin Moore, A. M., of Boston,..................	" 1861.

Honorary Vice-Presidents.

Hon.	Millard Fillmore, LL. D., of Buffalo, N. Y., ...	Feb. 1855.
Hon.	Lewis Cass, LL. D., of Detroit, Mich.,.............	" 1855.
Hon.	Elijah Hayward, A. B., of Columbus, O.,.........	" 1855.
Hon.	John Wentworth, of Chicago, Ill.,................	" 1855.
*Rev.	John Lauris Blake, D. D., of Orange, N. J.,......	Jan. 1856, to July 1857
Hon.	Samuel Breck, of Philadelphia, Pa.,..............	" 1856.
	Sebastian Ferris Streeter, A. M., of Baltimore, Md.	" 1856.
	Edward Kidder, Esq., of Wilmington, N. C.,......	" 1856.
Rev.	Thomas Smyth, D. D., of Charleston, S. C.,......	" 1856.
Hon.	Ballard Smith, of Cannelton, Ind.,...............	" 1856.
	Cyrus Woodman, A. M., of Mineral Point, Wis.,...	" 1856.
Rt. Rev.	Henry W. Lee, D. D., of Davenport, Iowa,.....	" 1856.
	*Andrew Randall, M. D., of San Francisco, Cal.,...	" 1856, to July 1856
Hon.	Joseph C. Hornblower, LL. D., of Newark, N. J.,..	" 1858.

Corresponding Secretaries.

Samuel G. Drake, A. M., of Boston,.............. Jan. 1845, to Jan. 1850
Nathaniel B. Shurtleff, M. D. of Boston,.......... " 1850, to " 1851
Samuel G. Drake, A. M., of Boston,.............. " 1851, to " 1858
Rev. Samuel H. Riddel, A. B., of Boston,.............. " 1858, to " 1859
John Ward Dean, of Boston,..................... " 1859, to " 1862
Rev. Caleb Davis Bradlee, A. M., of Roxbury, ... " 1862.

Assistant Corresponding Secretary.

John Ward Dean, of Boston,..................... Sept. 1858, to Jan. 1859

Recording Secretaries.

John Wingate Thornton, A. M., of Boston,....... Jan. 1845, to Mar. 1846
Rev. Samuel H. Riddel, A. B., of Boston,............... Apr. 1846, to Jan. 1851
*Charles Mayo, Esq., of Boston,.................. Jan. 1851, to " 1856
Hon. Francis Brinley, A. M., of Boston,................ " 1856, to " 1857
David Pulsifer, Esq., of Boston,.................. " 1857, to Aug. 1857
John Ward Dean, of Boston,..................... Aug. 1857, to Jan. 1858
William M. Cornell, M. D., of Boston,............ Jan. 1858, to " 1859
Rev. Caleb Davis Bradlee, A. M., of North Cambridge,.. " 1859, to " 1862
Edward F. Everett, A. B., of Charlestown,........ " 1862.

Assistant Recording Secretary.

Edward F. Everett, A. B., of Charlestown,........ Jan. 1861, to Jan. 1862

Treasurers.

William Henry Montague, Esq., of Boston,....... Jan. 1845, to Jan. 1851
Frederic Kidder, Esq., of Boston,................ " 1851, to " 1855
John Ward Dean, of Boston,..................... " 1855, to " 1857
Isaac Child, Esq., of Boston, ... " 1857, to " 1860
Hon. George W. Messinger, of Boston,................ " 1860, to " 1861
William B. Towne, Esq., of Brookline,............ " 1861.

Historiographers.

Joseph Palmer, M. D., of Boston,................. Jan. 1856, to Jan. 1862
William B. Trask, of Dorchester,... .... " 1862.

Librarians.

J. Wingate Thornton, A. M., of Boston,.......... Apr. 1845, to Jan. 1846
Edmund Bachelder Dearborn, Esq., of Boston,.... Jan. 1846, to " 1849
David Pulsifer, Esq., of Boston, ... " 1849, to " 1851
Thomas Bellows Wyman, Jr., Esq., of Charlestown, " 1851, to " 1852
William Blake Trask, Esq., of Dorchester,........ " 1852, to Aug. 1854
Rev. Luther Farnham, A. M., of Boston,.............. Aug. 1854, to July 1856
Thomas B. Wyman, Jr., Esq., of Charlestown,.... Sep. 1856, to Jan. 1858
Edward Holden, Esq., of Roxbury,.......... .... Jan. 1858, to " 1859
William Blake Trask, Esq., of Dorchester,........ " 1859, to " 1861
John H. Sheppard, A. M., of Boston,............ " 1861.

Directors.

*†Charles Ewer, Esq., of Boston,..... .... Jan. 1845, to Jan. 1850
*†Lemuel Shattuck, Esq., of Boston,................ " 1845, to " 1850
†Samuel G. Drake, A. M., of Boston,...... ...... " 1845, to " 1850
†J. Wingate Thornton, A. M., of Boston,.......... " 1845, to Mar. 1846
†William H. Montague, Esq., of Boston, ... " 1845, to Jan. 1851
†Rev. Samuel H. Riddel, A. B., of Boston,............. Apr. 1846, to " 1851
†Rev. Joseph B. Felt, LL. D., of Boston,................ Jan. 1850, to " 1853
†Rev. Lucius R. Paige, D. D., of Cambridge,..... ..... " 1850, to " 1851
†Nathaniel B. Shurtleff, M. D., of Boston,.......... " 1850, to " 1853

†Samuel G. Drake, A. M., of Boston,	Jan. 1851, to Jan. 1859
*†Charles Mayo, Esq., of Boston,	" 1851, to " 1856
†Frederic Kidder, Esq , of Boston,	" 1851, to " 1855
†William Whiting, A. M., of Roxbury,	" 1853, to " 1858
†Hon. Timothy Farrar, A. M., of Boston,	" 1853, to " 1858
†John Ward Dean, of Boston,	" 1855, to " 1857
†Hon. Francis Brinley, A. M., of Boston,	" 1856, to " 1857
†David Pulsifer, Esq., of Boston,	" 1857, to Aug. 1857
†Isaac Child, Esq., of Boston,	" 1857, to Jan. 1860
†John Ward Dean, of Boston,	Aug. 1857, to " 1858
†Hon. Francis Brinley, A. M., of Boston,	Jan. 1858, to " 1859
†Rev. Samuel H. Riddel, A. B., of Boston,	" 1858, to " 1859
†William M. Cornell, M. D., of Boston,	" 1858, to " 1859
†Almon D. Hodges, Esq., of Roxbury,	" 1859, to " 1861
†Hon. Charles Hudson, A. M., of Boston,	" 1859, to " 1861
John Ward Dean,‡ of Boston,	" 1859.
†Rev. Caleb Davis Bradlee, A M , of North Cambridge,	" 1859.
†Hon. George W. Messinger, of Boston,	" 1860, to Jan. 1861
†Winslow Lewis, M. D., of Boston,	" 1861.
Rev. Martin Moore,‡ A. M., of Boston,	" 1861.
†William B. Towne, Esq., of Brookline,	" 1861.
John H. Sheppard, A. M.,§ of Boston,	July 1861.
†Edward F. Everett, A. B., of Charlestown,	Jan. 1862.
†Rev. Joseph B. Felt, LL. D., of Salem,	" 1862.
†William Whiting, A. M., of Roxbury,	" 1862.
†Samuel G. Drake, A. M., of Boston,	" 1862.
†Almon D. Hodges, Esq., of Roxbury.	" 1862.
†William B. Trask, Esq., of Dorchester,	" 1862.
†Frederic Kidder, Esq., of Boston,	" 1862.
†Jeremiah Colburn, Esq., of Brookline,	" 1862.
†William Reed Deane, Esq., of Brookline,	" 1862.
Joseph Palmer, M. D., of Boston,	" 1862.
Hon. George W. Messinger, of Boston,	" 1862.
John Barstow, Esq., of Providence, R. I.,	" 1862.

Secretaries of the Directors.

†J. Wingate Thornton, A. M., of Boston,	Jan. 1845, to Mar. 1846
†Rev. Samuel H. Riddel, A. B., of Boston,	Apr. 1846, to Jan. 1851
Nathaniel B. Shurtleff, M. D., of Boston,	Jan. 1851, to " 1853
*†Charles Mayo, Esq., of Boston,	" 1853, to June 1855
John Ward Dean, of Boston,	June 1855, to Jan. 1856
†Hon. Francis Brinley, A. M., of Boston,	Jan. 1856, to " 1857
†David Pulsifer, Esq., of Boston,	" 1857, to Aug. 1857
†John Ward Dean, of Boston,	Aug. 1857, to Jan. 1858
†William M. Cornell, M. D., of Boston,	Jan. 1858, to " 1859
†Rev. Caleb Davis Bradlee, A. M., of North Cambridge,	" 1859, to Feb. 1861
Edward F. Everett, A. B., of Charlestown,	Feb. 1861.

Publishing Committee.

*Charles Ewer, Esq., of Boston,	Mar. 1847, to Jan. 1851
Nathaniel B. Shurtleff, M. D., of Boston,	" 1847, to " 1849
Rev. Samuel H. Riddel, A. B., of Boston,	" 1847, to " 1851
*David Hamblen, Esq., of Boston,	Jan. 1849, to Oct. 1855
*†William T. Harris, A. M., of Cambridge,	Feb. 1849, to " 1849
Rev. Joseph B. Felt, LL. D., of Boston,	Jan. 1850, to July 1852
Nathaniel B. Shurtleff, M. D , of Boston,	" 1850, to Jan. 1851
Rev. Lucius R. Paige, D. D., of Cambridge,	" 1850, to " 1851
Charles Deane, A. M., of Boston,	" 1851, to Oct. 1851
J Wingate Thornton, A. M., of Boston,	" 1851, to Mar. 1852

‡ Ex-officio till Jan. 1862. § By invitation of the Board till Jan. 1862.

*William T. Harris, A. M., of Cambridge,	Jan. 1851,	to Oct. 1851
Frederic Kidder, Esq., of Boston,	Oct. 1851,	to " 1855
Hon. Timothy Farrar, A. M., of Boston and Dorchester,	Nov. 1851,	to Dec. 1854
William B. Trask, Esq , of Dorchester,	Apr. 1852,	to Oct. 1853
*Charles Mayo, Esq., of Boston,	Oct. 1852,	to " 1853
Rev. William Jenks, D. D., of Boston,	" 1853,	to " 1858
Lyman Mason, A. M., of Boston,	" 1853,	to Dec. 1854
Rev. John Ward Dean, of Boston,	Dec. 1854.	
William Read Deane, Esq., of Brookline,	" 1854,	to Oct. 1856
*Lemuel Shattuck, Esq., of Boston,	" 1854,	to " 1856
Rev. Alonzo Hall Quint, A. M., of Jamaica Plain,	Oct. 1855,	to " 1856
James Spear Loring, Esq., of Boston,	" 1855,	to " 1856
Hon. Francis Brinley, A. M., of Boston,	" 1856,	to " 1858
Charles H. Morse, Esq., of Cambridgeport,	" 1856,	to " 1858
William H. Whitmore, Esq., of Boston,	" 1856,	to Nov. 1861
Hon. Timothy Farrar, A. M , of Boston,	Oct. 1857,	to Oct. 1858
William B. Trask, Esq., of Dorchester,	" 1858.	
Hon. Charles Hudson, A. M., of Lexington,	Nov. 1861.	
Rev. Elias Nason, A. M., of Exeter, N. H.,	" 1861.	
George W. Chase, Esq., of Haverhill,	" 1861.	

Committee on Donations and Exchanges.

James S. Loring, Esq., of Boston,	May 1850,	to Jan. 1852
Charles J. F. Binney, Esq., of Boston,	" 1850,	to " 1852
Hon. Amasa Walker, A. M., of North Brookfield,	Jan. 1852,	to " 1854
John G. Locke, Esq., of Boston,	" 1852,	to " 1853
James S. Loring, Esq., of Boston,	" 1853,	to " 1854

Committee on the Library and Room.

Isaac Child, Esq , of Boston,	Jan. 1852,	to Jan. 1856
*Artemas Simonds, Esq., of Boston,	" 1852,	to Oct. 1854

Committee on the Library.

‡Thomas B. Wyman, Jr., Esq , of Charlestown,	Jan. 1856,	to Jan. 1858
Charles H. Morse, Esq., of Cambridgeport,	" 1856,	to " 1857
William H. Whitmore, Esq., of Boston,	" 1856,	to " 1857
William B. Trask, Esq., of Dorchester.	" 1856,	to " 1858
†Rev. Luther Farnham, A. M., of Boston,	" 1856,	to July 1856
Dean Dudley, Esq., of Boston,	Oct. 1856,	to Jan. 1858
Rev. Caleb D. Bradlee, A. M., of North Cambridge,	Jan. 1857,	to " 1858
Sylvester Bliss, Esq., of Roxbury,	" 1857,	to " 1858
Thomas J. Whittemore, Esq., of Cambridge,	" 1858,	to " 1859
William Makepeace, Esq., of Boston,	" 1858,	to " 1859
Horace G. Barrows, M. D., of Boston,	" 1858,	to " 1859
Edward S. Rand, Jr., A. M., of Dedham,	" 1858,	to " 1859
†Edward Holden, Esq , of Roxbury,	" 1858,	to " 1859
Rev. Alonzo H. Quint, A. M., of Jamaica Plain,	" 1859,	to " 1861
Samuel Burnham, Esq., of Jamaica Plain,	" 1859,	to " 1861
Thomas Waterman, Esq., of Boston,	" 1859.	
J. Gardner White, Esq., of Boston,	" 1859,	to Jan. 1861
†William B. Trask, Esq., of Dorchester,	" 1859,	to " 1861
Frederic Kidder, Esq., of Boston,	" 1861,	to " 1862
Rev. James Thurston, A. M., of Belmont,	" 1861,	to " 1862
William S. Appleton, A. B., of Boston,	" 1861.	
†John H. Sheppard, A. M., of Boston,	" 1861.	
Jeremiah Colburn, Esq., of Brookline,	" 1862.	
Rev. Abner Morse, A. M., of Boston,	" 1862.	

‡Ex-officio from Sept. 1856 to Jan. 1858. § Ex-officio since Jan. 1861.

Committee on Finance.

Gen.	Samuel Andrews, of Roxbury,	Jan. 1852,	to Jan. 1856
	*David Hamblen, Esq., of Boston,	" 1852,	to Nov. 1855
*	Samuel Nicolson, Esq., of Boston,	" 1856,	to Jan. 1857
Col.	Samuel Swett, A. M., of Boston,	" 1856,	to " 1857
	Nathaniel Whiting, Esq., of Watertown,	" 1856,	to " 1857
Hon.	George W. Messinger, of Boston,	" 1856,	to " 1857
	†John W. Dean, of Boston,	" 1856,	to " 1857
	John W. Parker, Esq., of Roxbury,	" 1857,	to " 1858
	Charles H. Morse, Esq., of Cambridgeport,	" 1857,	to " 1858
Hon.	William Makepeace, Esq., of Boston,	" 1857,	to " 1858
	Thomas J. Whittemore, Esq., of Cambridge,	" 1857,	to " 1858
	†Isaac Child, Esq., of Boston,	" 1857,	to " 1860
	Sylvester Bliss, Esq., of Roxbury,	" 1858,	to " 1859
	William E. Baker, Esq., of Boston,	" 1858,	to " 1861
	Jacob Q. Kettelle, A. B., of Boston,	" 1858,	to " 1859
	C. Benj. Richardson, Esq., of Boston,	" 1858,	to Nov. 1858
	William Makepeace, Esq., of Boston,	" 1859,	to Jan. 1860
	Jeremiah Colburn, Esq., of Boston,	" 1859,	to " 1862
	Thomas J. Whittemore, Esq., of Cambridge,	" 1859.	
	§William B. Towne, Esq., of Brookline,	" 1860.	
Hon.	George W. Messinger,* of Boston,	Jan. 1860.	
	J. Tisdale Bradlee, Esq., of Boston,	" 1861.	
	Frederic Kidder, Esq., of Boston,	" 1862.	

Committee on Lectures and Essays.

Rev.	Martin Moore, A. M , of Boston,	Mar. 1860,	to Jan. 1861
Rev.	Lucius R. Paige, D. D., of Cambridge,	" 1860,	to " 1861
	William Reed Deane, Esq., of Brookline,	" 1860.	
Rev.	Frederic W. Holland, A. M., of Dorchester,	" 1860.	
	Thomas Cushing, A. M., of Boston,	" 1860.	
Rev.	Washington Gilbert, A. M., of West Newton,	Jan. 1861.	
	J. Gardner White, Esq., of Boston,	" 1861.	

Trustees of the Bond Fund and Property.

Almon D. Hodges, Esq., of Roxbury,	July 1859.
Frederic Kidder, Esq., of Boston,	" 1859.
John Ward Dean, of Boston,	" 1859.

Trustees of the Barstow Fund.

William B. Towne, Esq., of Brookline,	May 1862.
A. D. Hodges, Esq., of Roxbury,	" 1862.
J. Tisdale Brodlee, Esq., of Boston,	" 1862.

www.ingramcontent.com/pod-product-compliance
Lightning Source LLC
LaVergne TN
LVHW020638110826
845149LV00004B/1263

* 9 7 8 1 4 1 8 1 9 0 6 5 1 *